LAURE GUYET – previously a professional stylist – turned to the teaching of sewing and dressmaking, as she is passionate about sharing her knowledge with young and older enthusiasts alike! She supports her students in understanding how to use a sewing machine to bring their creative ideas to life.

Laure sees the promotion of sewing, the understanding of different fabrics and the construction of a garment as essential to her teaching practice.

Laure works in Paris, France.

Find Laure on Instagram: @laure.guyet

Also in the series:

9781800921634

Laure Guyet

THE
DRESSMAKING
Companion

SEARCH PRESS

CONTENTS

Introduction...5

PART ONE: Sewing machine and sewing equipment.........7

Sewing machine anatomy...8
Threading the machine 12
Settings 23
Equipment and maintenance..30
Cutting 38
Marking aids 40
Ironing..42

PART TWO: Fabrics and patterns...................................45

Fabrics 46
Patterns..74

PART THREE: Sewing techniques *83*

Hand sewing *84*

Seams *94*

Hems *100*

Bias binding *105*

Piping *108*

Ease *110*

Pleats and darts *114*

Gathers *120*

Buttonholes *121*

Zips (zippers) *124*

Necklines and openings *130*

Collars *136*

Pockets *140*

Index *150*

Acknowledgements *152*

Introduction

I have written this companion with the aim of helping anyone who is embarking on dressmaking for the first time, but also as a handy reference for those who are more experienced and might occasionally have a few questions about sewing clothes. I have tried to ensure that this book covers all the sewing essentials too.

Do *you* have a question? Are you unsure of the meaning of a particular term? Are you stuck on a project? Need help choosing a fabric? I hope you will find the answers to your questions in this book!

This book not only contains the basics of dressmaking; it's also a good place to record your own comments and discoveries.

Over to you!

Laure

Part One

Sewing machine and sewing equipment

Sewing machine anatomy

1. Stitch selection control.
2. Stitch length control.
3. Thread tension control.
4. Stitch width control and, consequently, needle position control (not all machines have this).
5. Reverse control lever (for backstitching at the beginning and end of a line of stitches).
6. Horizontal spool pin (on some models of sewing machine it may be vertical).
7. Bobbin winder spindle.

8. Bobbin winder stop (indicates when the bobbin is full).
9. Hole to insert a second spool pin.
10. Bobbin winder thread guide.
11. Top thread guide.
12. Thread cutter.
13. Removable arm/accessory box.
14. Front cover plate (remove to change the light bulb).
15. Thread take-up lever (also known as the hook)
16. Needle thread guide.

Disclaimer

Do read the manual for your particular sewing machine to fully understand the various parts: makes and models inevitably differ.

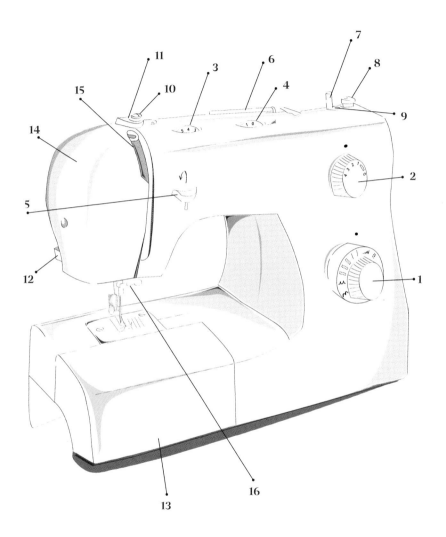

Presser bar

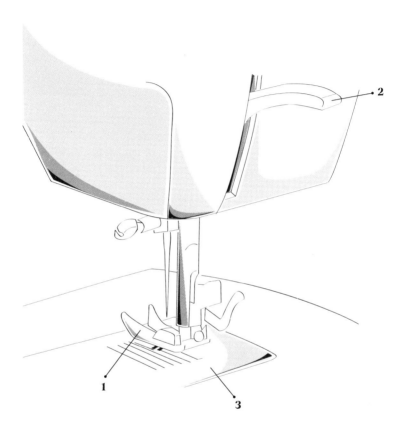

1. Presser foot.
2. Presser foot lever.
3. Needle plate.

Hand wheel

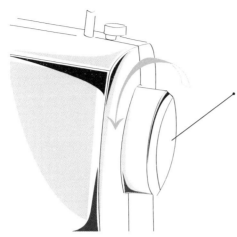

The wheel allows you to raise and lower the needle manually. It is important to always turn the wheel towards you, as this is the direction in which your machine operates.

Power switch

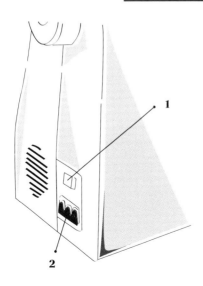

1. Power switch, to turn the sewing machine on and off. When you press the switch, the light illuminates your machine's needle plate.
2. Socket for pedal cable (rheostat).

Threading the machine

Winding the bobbin

First step before you start to sew: wind the bobbin!

1 Place your spool of thread on the spool pin. Pull the thread out from the spool and under the little hook.

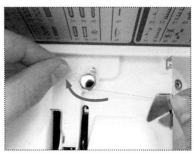

2 Pull the thread towards the round metal thread guide on the left of the machine, then between the two discs.

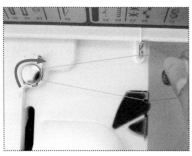

3 Bring it back around the disc then back towards the bobbin winder spindle.

4 Clip the bobbin to its spindle and insert the end of the thread up through the small hole located on the top of the bobbin, or wind a little of your thread directly around the bobbin from behind and in a clockwise direction.

5 Click the bobbin to the right, then turn on your machine. Apply gentle pressure to the pedal to allow the bobbin to fill.

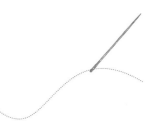

Top threading

1 Place your spool of thread on the spool pin then draw out the thread, taking it under a small hook or behind the metal thread guide (this will depend on your model of sewing machine).

2 Feed it down through the right-hand slot.

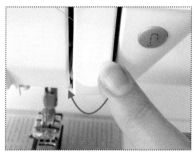

3 Bring it back up through the left-hand slot.

4 At the top, you will find a hook (the thread take-up lever). If you cannot see it, turn the hand wheel until it appears.

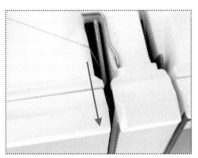

5 Keeping the tension on your thread, slip it through this hook from right to left.

6 Bring your thread back down (through the same slot), then trap it behind the needle thread guide. Then thread your needle: the thread goes from front to back.

7 Finally take your thread under the presser foot, towards the back of the machine.

Threading the bobbin (automatic)

On some machines, you will find you can see into the bobbin case from above, next to the needle plate. This allows you to keep an eye on how much thread remains on the bobbin.

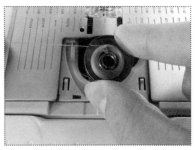

1 Remove the bobbin compartment cover plate by sliding it towards you, or by using a button on the right (depending on your model of sewing machine).

2 Position your bobbin in the compartment, ensuring that the end of the thread runs to the left of the bobbin. The bobbin should then turn in an anti-clockwise direction.

3 Holding the bobbin in place with your finger, pull on the thread to feed it into the tension spring. You should be able to see a small notch, through which you need to guide the thread.

4 Next, bring the thread to the left then upwards.

5 On some sewing machine models you can insert the thread as far as a thread cutter; this system is found on models with an automatic threading feature. Take the thread through the channel as shown.

Replace the cover of the bobbin compartment.

Threading using a bobbin case

A more traditional method, this mechanism often looks a bit scary, but it is not as complicated to thread as it initially seems. The bobbin case is hidden behind your machine's removable arm.

1 Take off the removable arm so you can access the bobbin mechanism.

2 Take the bobbin case and, holding it in one hand, drop in the bobbin. Make sure that when you pull on the thread, it turns clockwise.

3 Feed the thread through the slot and under the 'tongue' (tension spring) on the left.

4 Pull the thread until it appears in the opening. Pull out a length of thread.

5 Replace the case in the mechanism, ensuring that the hook points upwards. As you push it in, you should hear a little 'click' to indicate that it is properly engaged.

Picking up the bobbin thread

On sewing machines that do not have an automatic threading feature, you will need to pick up the bobbin thread yourself.

Your top thread should already be threaded through the machine, and you may need to adjust the tension to pick up the bobbin thread successfully. See page 29 for more on this.

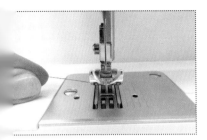

1 Holding the thread from the needle out to the left with one hand, turn the hand wheel towards you with the other hand.

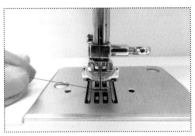

2 The needle will move downwards to pick up the bobbin thread.

3 Continue to turn the hand wheel towards you to bring the needle back up, and keep an eye on the thread take-up lever. Stop turning the hand wheel when the lever reaches the uppermost point.

4 Look under the presser foot (if necessary, pull the thread from the needle that you are holding gently upwards): a loop of thread will appear.

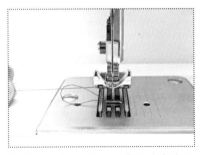

5 Slip an unpicker or a pin through the loop to help bring it up.

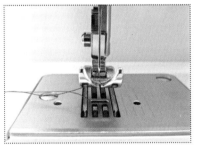

6 Pull upwards to bring out the end of the loop. You now have two threads: one from the needle and the other from the bobbin.

Needle threader

Some machines are fitted with a needle threader, which will allow you to pass your thread through the eye of the needle more easily.

1 Bring down the needle threader arm (keep it down throughout the process), then pass your thread under the hook on the left.

2 Bring your thread round in front of the hook and pull it across the front of the eye of your needle.

3 Release the needle threader so it goes back up. Your thread will have formed a loop coming out of the back of the eye of the needle.

4 Pull on this loop – your needle is threaded!

Settings

Backstitch – reversing stitch direction

What is it for?

- When you are sewing by hand, you might tie a knot to anchor your thread at the start and end of a seam – using a machine, backstitching means you sew over your stitches and strengthen your seam.
- When you are sewing a seam between two pieces of fabric, it is important to think of securing it so it does not come apart.

When to use?

At the beginning and end of a seam.

✴ ✴ ✴ *What not to do!* ✴ ✴ ✴

Do not use this function to sew backwards.

The different stitches

Here is a selection of the most common stitches found on sewing machines.
These can differ with each machine.

1. Straight stitch

Used for sewing pieces together and top-stitching (suitable for woven fabrics).

2. Triple straight stitch and straight stretch stitch

Used for sewing together stretch fabrics and knits. If you use a standard straight stitch with these types of fabric, seams can split when you put on your clothes. Triple straight stitch and straight stretch stitch allow you to sew seams that retain their stretch properties. You use the same thread – no need for elastic thread.

3. Zigzag stitch

Used to reinforce a seam, or to overlock edges to prevent the fabric from fraying. It can also be used for decoration or to insert lace.

4. Blind hem stitch

Used to sew invisible hems on woven fabrics.

5. Blind hem stretch stitch

Used to form invisible hems on stretch fabrics.

6. Multi-stitch zigzag stitch

For sewing elastic or darning your clothes.

7. Overlock stitch

Enables you to sew and finish a seam in one operation.

8. Double overlock stitch

Enables you to sew and finish a seam in one operation on stretch fabrics.

9. Buttonhole stitch

This stitch allows you to make buttonholes on your garments.

10. Feather stitch

Basically a decorative stitch but also useful for sewing together quilted fabrics.

11. Scallop stitch

A fancy, decorative stitch.

Stitch selector

What is it for?

The stitch selector control allows you to choose the stitch you want to use for your sewing (straight stitch, zigzag, blind hem, buttonhole, etc.). Some models of sewing machine offer a greater range of possibilities than others.

When to use

Select your stitch before starting to sew.

✳ ✳ ✳ *What not to do!* ✳ ✳ ✳

Do not change stitch while your needle is still in the fabric – the needle could break!

Stitch length control

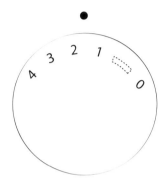

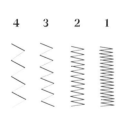

— — — —	4
— — — — —	3
- - - - - - - - - ·	2
- - - - - - - - - - - -	1
⌐ - - - - - ¬	**Buttonhole**
–	0

4	3	2	1

What is it for?

This allows you to select the stitch length you want. The length generally ranges from 1mm to 4mm. If the stitch is too small, your fabric may pucker – it is not always because there is a tension problem!

You can also decide how long you want your stitches to be on the basis of how you want any visible seams to look.

When to use

Select your stitch length before starting to sew.

✳ ✳ ✳ *What not to do!* ✳ ✳ ✳

Do not change stitch length while you are sewing.

Stitch width control

What is it for?

This allows you to adjust the stitch width. It does not have any effect on the straight stitch itself, but allows your needle to shift to the left or right depending on your model of machine. If your machine does not have this gauge, your needle position will be adjusted automatically when you select a stitch other than straight stitch. Machines with this function are easy to use but do not allow you to adjust your stitch as precisely as you may want.

When to use

For all stitches other than straight stitch, allowing you to enlarge or 'flatten' your design.

❋ ❋ ❋ *What not to do!* ❋ ❋ ❋

Do not adjust while your needle is still in the fabric – the needle could break!

Thread tension control

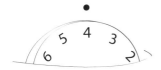

What is it for?

This should be adjusted according to the thickness of your fabric. For the majority of textiles you might use, your machine tension will be set to 4 (or automatic), but it is important to do a test run on a sample of your fabric to check that the tension is correct.

When to use

If thread tension is too tight it can break the thread easily and can also cause fine fabric to pucker. In this case, decrease the tension by turning the gauge to a lower number.

Likewise, if thread tension is too loose, stitches will be untidy and loose loops of thread may form. In this case, increase the tension by turning the gauge to a higher number.

❋ ❋ ❋ ***What not to do!*** ❋ ❋ ❋

Do not make adjustments without first sewing a test sample on the fabric!

Tip

You may sometimes find that, although you are getting fairly neat stitches on both the top and bottom of your fabric, the underneath thread is coming up between each stitch. This appears as a straight line, a dot, a straight line, a dot, etc. If you run your finger over the seam, you can feel the 'dot' and the seam is not smooth. This indicates a problem with bobbin thread tension. Do not adjust the top thread tension, but find the adjustment screw on your bobbin case and tighten gradually, testing as you go. For machines where you can see the bobbin compartment from above, you need to remove the needle plate, take out the bobbin case and identify the screw with the yellow or green wax cover.

For machines where the bobbins are inserted underneath, take out the bobbin case and tighten the screw on top of the tension tab.

Equipment and maintenance

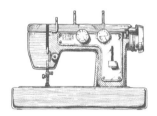

Machine maintenance

It is important to remember to clean your sewing machine from time to time. Use a small brush to prevent dust and pieces of thread from collecting in the bobbin mechanism or in the thread-guide slots.

Lubricate your machine occasionally, following the manufacturer's instructions. This is particularly important for mechanical machines, where you can take off the cap to apply a few drops of oil to the central shaft.

Warning! Always use the oil specifically formulated for sewing machines and sold in specialist shops.

It is advisable to have electronic machines serviced by a professional every three years.

With mechanical machines, you can change the bulb yourself if the filament blows. To do this, remove your sewing machine cover and check whether the bulb has a screw or bayonet fitting.

Tip

It is advisable to keep your sewing machine under a cover or in a cupboard so it does not get too dusty. It is also a good idea to keep a small piece of fabric under the presser foot to 'plug' the openings around the feed teeth and prevent dust from accumulating inside the mechanism.

The different needles

Consider whether or not the fabric you are using will require a change of needle: it is a simple little step towards a smoother sewing experience!

1. Universal needle
This needle will pierce different kinds of fabrics.
It has a slightly rounded tip but is sharper than the point of a jersey needle. It will come as standard with your sewing machine.

2. Denim needle
This needle will pierce thicker fabrics such as denim. It is much thicker than a universal needle, and its point will pierce all the layers of fabric more easily.

3. Stretch needle
A stretch needle has a rounded tip, especially designed to prevent skipped stitches. It is useful for sewing very stretchy knits and elastics.

4. Ballpoint needle / jersey needle

A ballpoint, or jersey, needle is recommended for sewing knitted fabric; its round tip allows it to pierce the fabric without damaging its fibres.

5. Double needle / twin needle

The double/twin needle lets you sew two rows of parallel stitching on the right side of the fabric, creating a zigzag on the wrong side.

It is used on all types of fabric, but make sure you use one especially for jersey if you are sewing knitted fabric.

To get started, insert the second spool holder (small spindle) that comes with your machine. It is often inserted on the top right of the machine, either in a little spindle-shaped hole, or near the bobbin winder spindle. Next, thread your second thread like the first (it passes through all the same places), then thread one thread in the right-hand needle and the other in the left-hand needle.

Threads

Fabric weight	Fabric type
Fine fabric	Batiste, voile, crêpe, etc.
Medium-weight fabric	Gaberdine, satin, modal, poplin, jersey, etc.
Heavy-weight fabric	Denim, twill, velvet, wool, etc.

Thread type	Thread weight	Needle size (European/ US)
Silk, cotton, polyester, foam	80–100	60–70 (60/8–70/10)
Cotton, polyester, fancy thread	50–80	80–90 (80/12–90/14)
Cotton, polyester	40–80	100–110 (100/16–110/18)

Presser feet

1. Standard foot

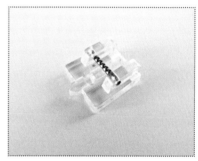

2. Concealed-zip (-zipper) foot

3. Zip (zipper) foot

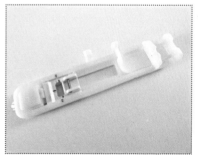

4. One-step buttonhole foot

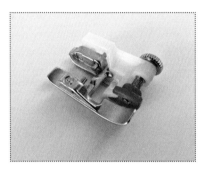

5. Blind hem foot

6. Rolled hem foot

7. Teflon foot

8. Button-sewing foot

Cutting

1. Thread cutter

For snipping threads. Smaller than scissors, they are ideal to have on hand near your machine.

2. Seam ripper or unpicker

This little device will be your best friend! It allows you to unpick stitches, open buttonholes and pull out threads.

3. Sewing scissors

A pair of sewing scissors is indispensable for cutting fabric properly. They are shaped such that the fabric remains flat as you cut.

4. Pinking shears

Useful for clipping seam allowances after you've stitches a seam, preventing edges from fraying. However, a pinked edge is never a substitute for one that has been overcast.

5. Embroidery scissors

Also known as 'stork scissors', they can be used to make small, neat, accurate cuts.

6. Rotary cutters

Rotary cutters are ideal for straight, precise cutting – use them to cut leather, and small pieces of work.

7. Tailor's awl/stiletto

Useful for marking specific points, making eyelets or positioning hardware and buttons.

Marking aids

1. Tailor's chalk – erasable pen – tailor's wax

The tailor's chalk or pen will allow you to transfer notches or any other markings you will need from the pattern to the fabric.

Tailor's waxes are best used on woollens, and disappear when ironed.

2. Carbon paper

Carbon paper, with the help of a tracing wheel (see below), will help you to transfer markings from the pattern on to the fabric. It is generally available in red, blue, yellow and white. Note that carbon paper can sometimes leave marks.

3. Tracing wheel

Used with carbon paper to transfer pattern lines, or to transfer darts to paper when pattern making.

4. Parrot ruler – pistol ruler

These French curved tracing rulers take their names from their shapes. The 'pistol' is normally longer and narrower, while the 'parrot' offers more rounded shapes.

These tools help you to draw accurate curves for necklines and armholes.

5. Quilting ruler

These flexible rulers are very practical for drawing your seam allowances and tracing patterns. Their gridlines mean you can also use them as set squares.

6. Tailor's ruler

A real multi-tasker! It has rounded edges, right angles, a straight edge for measuring, slots for marking folds, and markings for buttonholes and buttons of different diameters.

7. Sewing gauge

This small ruler allows you to measure in both centimetres and inches. It also has a sliding marker for marking hems and seam allowances.

Ironing

1. Iron

Keep it on and at the ready as you sew!
Regularly ironing your work as you sew it
together will ensure a better finish.

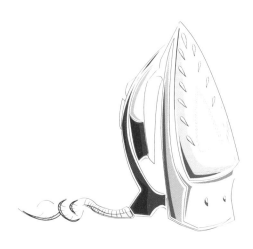

2. Sleeve board

This small version of an ironing board is used to iron narrow parts of garments such as sleeves or trouser legs.

3. Pressing ham / tailor's ham

Allows you to shape garment parts where needed (sleeves, for example). The shape prevents unwanted folds from forming.

4. Pressing cloth

A pressing cloth is a piece of damp cloth that you position over your fabric to protect it. It prevents the baseplate of the iron from being in direct contact with the fabric. Use with fragile fabrics or to prepare the pieces of fabric before you start work on the sewing machine.

Part Two

Fabrics and patterns

Fabrics

There are three main textile families:

1. Woven,
also referred to as fabrics.

2. Knitted,
generally known as wools and jerseys.

3. Non-woven,
often used as single-use textiles (such as tablecloths and other textiles used when entertaining) or used in industry as technological textiles (in the construction or automotive sector).

For clothing, we basically use woven and knitted fabrics.

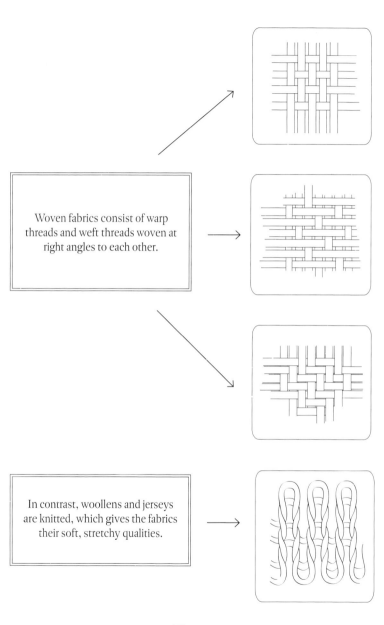

Woven fabrics consist of warp threads and weft threads woven at right angles to each other.

In contrast, woollens and jerseys are knitted, which gives the fabrics their soft, stretchy qualities.

Weave

The weave refers to the way in which the warp and weft threads cross each other.

✳ **_Plain weave:_** the simplest, where the weft threads pass alternately over and under the warp threads.

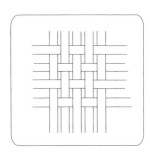

✳ **_Twill weave:_** twill weave forms diagonals and results in a more flexible fabric.

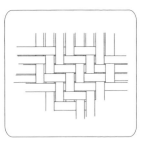

✳ **_Satin weave:_** the warp and weft threads cross further apart. The threads are evenly spaced out.

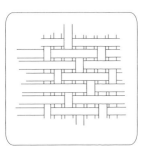

Treatments

After weaving, fabric can be treated in numerous ways.

✳ ***Milling:*** a process used to consolidate wool and felt fabric (they become more compact and water resistant).

✳ ***Napping:*** a process that gives the surface of a fabric a softer, fluffier finish.

✳ ***Coating:*** application of a substance to the textile to make it waterproof, give it a shine or change its appearance.

Tip

There is little point nowadays in thinking purely in terms of cotton, wool, silk, polyester, and so on. For example, take curtains, a pretty broderie-anglaise summer dress and a pair of jeans: they are all made of cotton, yet the finished product is not the same at all. Think of the thickness or weight (in grams, as for paper).

In our example, cotton is a fibre used to make the fabric, but the way in which it is then woven and treated differs, depending on the desired use.

This is why there is such a multitude of different fabrics, different names and combinations of different fibres.

Grain and bias

Grain

The grain is the direction in which the fabric has been woven or knitted.

The grain is always parallel to the selvedge (selvage) and runs in the direction of the warp yarns.

You will find an arrow marked 'GL' meaning 'grain line' on your patterns. This will help you position your pieces on the fabric.

Tip: how to identify the grain when there is no selvedge (selvage)

Stretch the fabric between your fingers:

✳ *If it does not give (and makes a rather dry, snapping sound), this is the grain.*

✳ *If the fabric stretches slightly (the fabric is more flexible), this is the direction of the weft yarn.*

Bias

The bias is the direction in which the fabric stretches the most and is most easily pulled out of shape. Unless your pattern specifically instructs you to do so, never position your pattern on the bias of the fabric, as it may stretch once cut.

COTTONS

POPLIN

A lightweight, silky-looking fabric, with fine horizontal ribs.

Used for:

Dresses, blouses and children's clothes.

Washing:

60° C (140° F).

Ironing:

Hot iron.

Gaberdine

A twill-woven fabric made of wool, cotton or synthetic fibre. It is a strong, quite stiff material.

Used for:

Coats, skirts, trousers and waterproofs.

Washing:

Dry-clean.

Ironing:

Hot iron.

CHAMBRAY

A soft cotton fabric with a dyed warp thread and a white weft thread. Chambray looks a little like denim, but is lighter and less closely woven.

Used for:

Shirts, dresses and summer trousers.

Washing:

60° C (140° F).

Ironing:

Very hot iron.

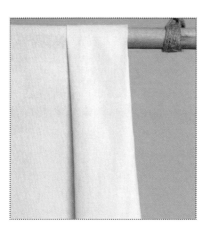

CAMBRIC

A fabric made from cotton or linen. Cambric is a very lightweight fabric that is soft to the touch.

Used for:

Lingerie, nightwear, tops and children's clothes.

Washing:

Hand-wash or 40° C (104° F).

Ironing:

Warm iron.

BRODERIE ANGLAISE

A fabric traditionally made from white cotton, with patterns formed by the small, embroidered holes. Small lengths are also sometimes used decoratively.

Used for:
Baby clothes, dresses and blouses.

Washing:
60° C (140° F).

Ironing:
Warm iron.

MOLESKIN

Moleskin is a heavy cotton fabric, with a short pile on one side, giving it a suede-like appearance.

Used for:
Jackets and trousers.

Washing:
40° C (104° F).

Ironing:
Hot iron.

DENIM

Its twill weave creates its characteristic diagonal ribbing. It was traditionally woven with a white weft thread and a coloured (often blue) warp thread. These days, it is much more commonly dyed.

Used for:

Jeans, jackets and shirts.

Washing:

30° C (86° F) to 60° C (140° F).

Ironing:

Hot iron.

CANVAS

Canvas is a very sturdy, close-woven, twill cotton fabric.

Used for:

Jeans, jackets, shirts and work overalls.

Washing:

40° C (104° F).

Ironing:

Hot iron.

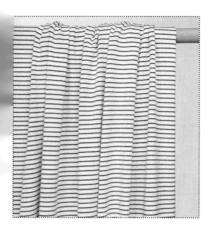

JERSEY COTTON

Knitted cotton fabric. The front (right side) of this fabric is different from the back (wrong side) – the right side is quite smooth and formed of 'V's, while the wrong side looks like waves. Jersey stretches in both directions although its elasticity is greater widthways.

Used for:

T-shirts, undergarments, skirts, dresses and sports clothing.

Washing:

30° C (86° F).

Ironing:

Warm iron.

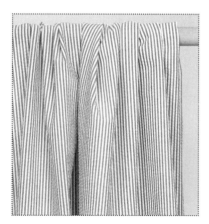

SEERSUCKER

This fabric alternates flat and puckered stripes. The puckered stripes are woven into the fabric and do not disappear upon ironing.

Used for:

Children's clothing, dresses.

Washing:

60° C (140° F).

Ironing:

No need to iron.

WOOLS

FLANNEL

Flannel is a plain- or twill-woven fabric, brushed on both sides to give a fuzzy finish. A key feature is how soft it is to the touch.

Used for:

Suits, jackets, trousers, nightwear.

Washing:

Hand-wash or dry-clean.

Ironing:

Hot iron.

CASHMERE

This magnificent fabric is woven from soft, luxurious goat's wool and is soft and silky in appearance.

Used for:

Suits, tailored jackets and coats.

Washing:

Hand-wash or dry-clean.

Ironing:

Do not iron.

TWEED

A fabric with a knobbly finish and thick weft. Made originally from pure wool, some modern tweeds are woven from a mixture of wool and cotton or synthetic fibres. It is the signature fabric of a major *haute couture* fashion brand!

Used for:

Suits, tailored jackets, coats and skirts.

Washing:

Dry-clean.

Ironing:

Warm iron with a damp pressing cloth.

MOHAIR

This fabric is made from the wool of angora goats. Nowadays, mohair is often mixed with sheep's wool.

Used for:

Suits, tailored jackets and coats.

Washing:

Hand-wash or dry-clean.

Ironing:

Warm iron with a damp pressing cloth.

ALPACA

Made from alpaca wool, often mixed with sheep's wool to reduce the cost. This very lightweight, very soft wool makes a luxurious and very expensive fabric.

Used for:

Coats.

Washing:

Dry-clean.

Ironing:

Warm iron.

SILKS AND LINEN

RAW SILK

Raw silk is obtained from the 'waste' discarded during the spinning process. Its knobbly surface texture makes it very distinctive.

Used for: Blouses, dresses and outfits for special occasions.

Washing: Dry-clean.

Ironing: Hot iron.

TAFFETA

Taffeta was initially a silk fabric, but nowadays is often made of synthetic fibre. It is a soft, plain-weave fabric with a crisp appearance. It has very fine ribs and a distinctive shine. Creases easily.

Used for: Wedding dresses and special-occasion outfits.

Washing: Dry-clean.

Ironing: Hot iron.

CRÊPE DE CHINE

The weave uses a taut thread, which gives this fabric its uneven surface texture. When cut on the bias, it drapes beautifully.

Used for: Blouses, dresses and lingerie.

Washing: Dry-clean.

Ironing: Warm iron.

GEORGETTE CRÊPE

This lightweight, sheer fabric looks like muslin, but is made of twisted threads which give it its grainy appearance.

Used for:

Scarves and dresses.

Washing:

Dry-clean.

Ironing:

Hot iron.

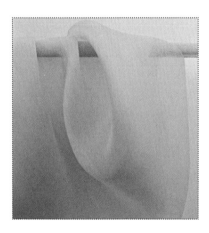

ORGANZA

A sheer, lightweight but crisp fabric.

Used for:

Interfacing and wedding dresses.

Washing:

Dry-clean or hand-wash.

Ironing:

Warm iron.

WASHED SILK

Obtained by washing silk so it loses its shine.

Used for:

Dresses, blouses.

Washing:

Dry-clean.

Ironing:

Warm iron.

LINEN CANVAS

Linen comes from the stalk of the flax plant, and is a sturdy fabric with a slightly coarse finish. It is particularly prone to creasing.

Used for:

Dresses, blouses and trousers.

Washing:

Hand-wash or dry-clean.

Ironing:

Very hot iron.

SYNTHETICS

ACRYLIC

A lightweight, woven or knitted fabric which has the same property as wool: it keeps you warm. Its name comes from the chemical process by which it is made: the polymerization of acrylonitrile.

Used for: Knitted garments and sports clothing.

Washing: Hand-wash.

Ironing: Hot iron.

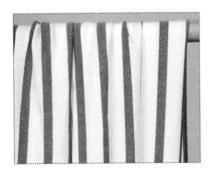

VISCOSE

A fabric made from wood pulp or cotton flock. Viscose is soft and drapes well.

Used for: Dresses, blouses and tops.

Washing: Hand-wash or machine-wash at 30° C (86° F).

Ironing: Hot iron.

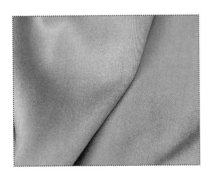

ACETATE

Made predominantly from chemicals, the fabric drapes well and has a slight shine.

Used for: Lingerie, lining and sports clothing.

Washing: Dry-clean.

Ironing: Warm iron.

MICROFIBRE

A close-woven fabric of very fine fibres, often made from polyester.

Used for: Dresses, blouses and tops.

Washing: Hand-wash or machine-wash at 30° C (86° F).

Ironing: Hot iron.

NYLON

A synthetic fibre made from products of mineral-based origin. Nylon is light and non-absorbent and can create static electricity.

Used for: Rainwear and skiwear.

Washing: Hand-wash.

Ironing: Warm iron.

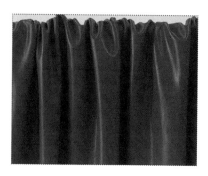

VINYL (SYNTHETIC LEATHER)

As its alternative names 'synthetic leather' or 'pleather' imply, it looks like leather.

Used for: Clothes, accessories and soft furnishings.

Washing: Cannot be washed, or even dry-cleaned. Wipe with a clean, non-abrasive cloth.

Ironing: Do not iron.

POLYESTER

A widely used synthetic fibre with a huge range of uses. Often mixed with other fibres such as wool and cotton.

Used for:

Dresses, tops, shirts, trousers, skirts and coats.

Washing:

Hand-wash or 30° C (86° F).

Ironing:

Warm iron.

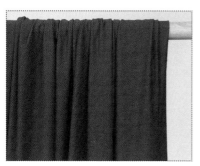

LYCRA

A very stretchy fabric. Often mixed with other fibres to increase a fabric's elasticity.

Used for:

Swimwear, lingerie and sports clothing.

Washing:

40° C (104° F).

Ironing:

Warm iron.

FUSIBLE AND NON-FUSIBLE INTERFACINGS

Iron-on, interfacing, fusible, interlining – it's a minefield!

Fusible interfacing and lining

Lining material and fusible interfacing are used in the same way. 'Interfacing' simply means using another layer of material to strengthen or stiffen that piece of the garment – a collar, a cuff or the hem of a coat, for example. However, lining is designed to be visible; interfacing is usually hidden between layers of fabric.

Nowadays, it is possible to buy fabrics with a fine coating of glue (on the wrong side of the fabric), which can be fused directly to the main fabric by pressing with an iron. This material is known as fusible interfacing, or Vlieseline® (trade name).

Choosing the right interfacing

As with fabrics, interfacing comes in a variety of weights: light, medium or heavy. Your choice will depend on your fabric or the finish you wish to achieve. You do not want to make the fabric too stiff, otherwise it will look and feel like cardboard!

1. Woven fusible interfacing

Ideal for clothing and accessories.

2. Non-woven fusible interfacing

More suitable for accessories or for backing smaller surface areas, such as a shirt collar or cuffs.

3. Mesh fusible interfacing

Specially designed for knitted and stretch fabrics, mesh fusible can also be used with woven fabrics. It is the most flexible and lightweight fusible.

4. Interlining

Not used so much in home sewing, it has traditionally been used for making high-class garments such as tailored jackets and coats.

These woven fabrics ensure that your garments hold their shape and hang well, and provide the best finish.

However, they are very time-consuming as you need to secure the interlining by hand-sewing it to the fabric.

5. Underlining

Using underlining means cutting out the pieces of your garment a second time in a soft, lightweight fabric. Underlining is applied directly under the fabric before using any interfacing.

It is a little like making a 'mould' of the garment in order to give structure to material that is too soft, or to reinforce a fragile fabric.

6. Lining

Lining is the last stage in making a garment. It gives a more finished look to what you have made by concealing the work on the wrong side.

It also has the advantage of providing structure to soft fabric (skirts or trousers) and, above all, it makes it easier to put on or take off a jacket!

Patterns

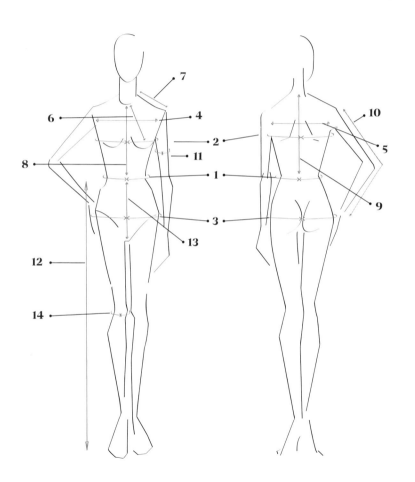

Measurements

It is important to check your measurements against the pattern size guide to avoid any unwanted surprises at a later stage. Dressmaking sizes do not necessarily correspond to the size you might go for when buying clothes in shops.

1. Waist
It is quite high! You need to find the narrowest point under your ribcage.

2. Bust
Pass the tape measure under your arms, straight across your back and round the fullest part of your chest.

3. Hips
The fullest part of the hips, around 22cm (8¾in) below the waist. The tape measure will go round approximately halfway down your buttocks.

4. Armpit to armpit (front)
Imagine that you do not have any arms (like a tailor's dummy) and position the tape measure from armpit to armpit.

5. Armpit to armpit (back)
As for the front – you will need someone to help you take this measurement.

6. Upper chest
Take the tape measure from the notch at the top of the sternum, between the collarbones, to the fullest part of the chest.

7. Shoulder length
Take the tape measure from the point where the neck meets the shoulder to the end of the shoulder.

8. Front waist
Take this measurement from the little notch at the top of the sternum, between the collarbones, to the waist.

9. Nape to waist

Take this measurement from the nape of the neck (where the back of your hair begins) to the waist.

10. Arm length

Bend your arm slightly so there will be enough give in your sleeves to ensure that you will be able to bend your arms.

11. Arm circumference

Simply measure round your arm at its fullest point.

12. Outside leg length

Waist to floor.

13. Rise length

A more difficult measurement to take: take the tape measure from your waist down to crotch level. Do not go too far – you are not measuring as far as the seam on your trousers.

14. Knee circumference

Flex your knee slightly and simply take the measurement around it.

After you have taken your measurements, refer to your pattern's measurement chart to choose the correct pattern size for you. If you find yourself between two sizes, it is best to opt for the larger one, then you can adjust your seams accordingly. Don't forget that it is always better to have too much fabric than too little!

There is no point in comparing your waist, bust and hip measurement directly by measuring the pattern pieces, as the pattern maker (depending on the pattern) will have included ease and allowances.

Vocabulary

Right side / wrong side
The right side is the side that will be on the outside of the finished garment, while the wrong side will be on the inside and not visible.

Bolt width
Width of the fabric between the two selvedges (selvages). The bolt width can vary between one roll of fabric and another.

Most common: 115cm (45in) and 150cm (60in); for certain fabrics (such as Liberty) between 110cm (43¼in) and 125cm (49¼in); and for soft furnishings 200cm (78¾in).

Selvedge (selvage)
The side edge(s) of the fabric. The selvedge (selvage) may be woven quite tightly, or frayed with small holes along its length. On some fabrics it takes the form of a white stripe bearing the manufacturer's name.

Seam allowance
The seam allowance is the amount added to the pattern to allow the pieces to be sewn together securely. It is the distance between the seamline and the fabric edge.

Seam
Stitched line joining two pieces of fabric together.

Cut on the fold
Fold the fabric and position the front or back midline of the pattern piece against the fold, to cut a single piece without a seam down the middle of the panel.

Notches
Notches are marks that help you align one pattern piece with another when sewing them together.

Markings
Pattern markings can indicate where to place elements such as buttons and press fasteners, or allow you to align two pattern pieces.

Tack or baste
A temporary hand-sewn seam to hold the pieces together before sewing on the machine or overlocker. The thread you use for tacking (basting) should contrast with the fabric so it is visible, and the stitches should be fairly widely spaced to make them easier to pick.

Reducing bulk

Trimming the seam allowance. You clip corners so they lie flat.

Overlocking

Overlocking allows you to sew two pieces together while also finishing the edges of the fabric so they do not fray.

Overcasting

Overcasting is a zigzag stitch that simply finishes the edges of the fabric so they do not fray.

Neckline

The opening at the top of the garment that goes around the neck.

Facing

A facing is a narrow piece of fabric identical to the part of the garment to be edged in shape, to add structure and help the garment lie flat. A facing is often sewn along a neckline or the top of a skirt and then folded over to the inside to finish the garment neatly.

Ease

Ease is the surplus fabric often included in a pattern to allow more movement when wearing the garment. For example, the top edge of the sleeve piece is generally bigger than the armhole so you can move your arm in the garment without stretching it.

Fold

Simply means fold the fabric along the line of the seam allowance. You make a fold to create a hem, for example.

Press open

Pressing a seam open means opening out the seam allowances on either side of the seamline.

Press to the side

Pressing to the side simply means folding both seam allowances to one side of the seamline.

Clip

This means making small cuts in the seam allowance, perpendicular to the edge of the fabric, to release any tension. Curves are often clipped so the fabric can be turned out or ironed without creasing or puckering.

Decatizing

This is the process of treating fabrics to prevent them from shrinking, and to give the chosen fabric more stability. There are various methods, but the easiest is to prewash the fabric before cutting it, in your washing machine.

Symbols

↓ 'On-fold' line
Fold the fabric and position the 'on fold' marking of the pattern against the fold so as to obtain a single symmetrical piece after cutting, without a seam down the middle.

Darts
These markings need to be transferred to your fabric to be sewn at a later stage. See page 118.

■ ● ✳ Markings
These markings can show where to place a button, a press fastener or two pieces together.

⊱ ├ Notches
Notches are marks to help you align one pattern piece with another when sewing them together.

→│ Folds
The arrow shows the direction in which you should fold your fabric when sewing together.

├────┤ Buttonhole / button loop

Seamline / size lines
You will select which size line to follow on the basis of your measurements. Each size (line on the pattern) is represented by a different colour or line style.

─○─ Right side of fabric

○─○ Wrong side of fabric

═══ Lengthening or shortening line
These lines allow you to adapt your pattern and ensure best possible fit. If you need to lengthen or shorten a piece, note how many centimetres (or inches) too long or short it is and divide this distance by the number of lines on the pattern to balance it out and retain the pattern's overall proportions.

Cutting diagram

The cutting diagram gives you guidance on how to lay out the pattern pieces on your fabric. The pattern will specify how much fabric you need and how the pieces should be laid out in order to waste as little fabric as possible.

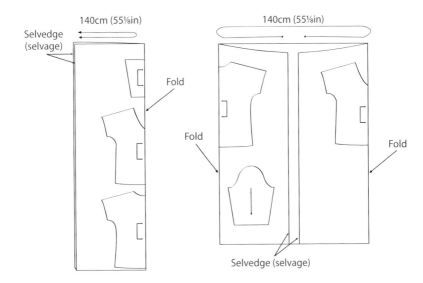

The left-hand cutting diagram, opposite, represents your length of fabric folded in half, selvedge to selvedge (selvage to selvage), with the various pattern pieces laid out on it.

Cutting diagrams sometimes show the fabric with the selvedges (selvages) folded to the centre so as to create a fold on each side (see the right-hand diagram, opposite). This is known as a 'gate fold'.

You should seek to follow the cutting diagram precisely in terms of how you position your pieces on the fabric.

✳ ✳ ✳ *Warning!* ✳ ✳ ✳

Selvedge to selvedge (selvage to selvage) means you fold the fabric in half along its width, matching the side (selvedge/selvage) edges. Do not confuse this with a fold from top to bottom.

Some patterns will provide more than one cutting diagram. Take time to look at the instructions: they will be for two different widths of cloth. These can vary depending on pattern sizes or style options.

Part Three

Sewing techniques

Hand sewing

Tacking or basting

What is it for?

Tacking (basting) stitches allow you to hold two pieces of fabric together temporarily before you sew them together on the machine.

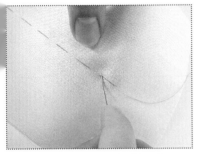

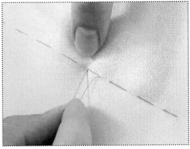

1 Insert your needle into the fabric from the wrong side, then bring it out on the right side. Draw the thread, leaving a 10cm (4in) tail on the wrong side. Form a stitch approximately 1cm (⅜in) in length.

2 Repeat at regular intervals, taking the needle up and down through the fabric and leaving an approximately 1cm (⅜in) gap between each stitch.

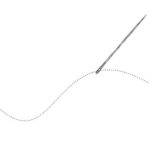

3 Continue tacking (basting) along the full length you wish to sew together.

Backstitch

What is it for?

Backstitch is stronger than tacking (basting) and holds your fabric pieces together more securely.

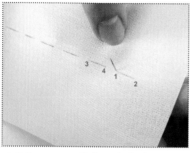

1 Bring your needle from the back to the front of the fabric at point 1.

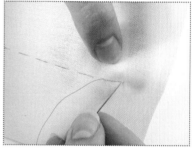

2 Take your needle back along the row of stitches and reinsert at point 2.

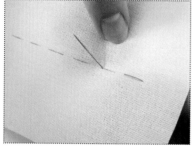

3 Bring your needle up again some distance beyond the initial stitch you have formed at point 3.

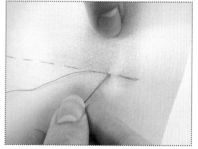

4 Take your needle back again and reinsert it at point 4.

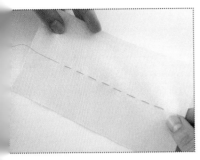

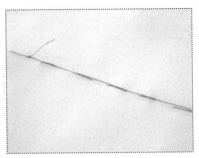

5 Repeat steps 1–4 as necessary to create a line of straight stitches on the right side of the fabric.

6 On the wrong side you will have an unbroken row of stitches.

Variation

For a stronger stitch, work backstitch
with no space between the stitches
on the right side.

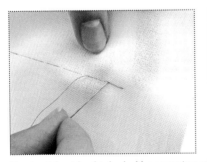

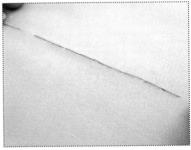

On the right side, this looks like a running stitch done on a sewing machine.

Slipstitch

What is it for?

This stitch is ideal if you need to sew something invisibly – from hems and bias binding to enclosing and joining seams. The steps below show you how to join two pieces of fabric together with slipstitch.

1 Prepare your two pieces of fabric by making a fold along one edge of each.

2 Slip your needle under the fold and bring it up through the folded edge of one of the two fabrics.

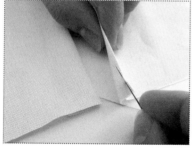

3 Then take your needle through the folded edge of the second piece of fabric in the same way, approximately 5mm (¼in) further on.

4 Repeat step 3 with the first piece of fabric.

5 Continue to sew the rest of the seam in the same way. Try to ensure the spacing of your stitches is regular.

6 Every few stitches, pull gently on the thread so the two folded edges come together.

7 Once you have finished the seam, your stitches will be invisible, even on the wrong side of the fabric.

Blind hem stitch

What is it for?
This stitch is generally used for sewing invisible hems.

1 Prepare your hem by folding it and pressing with an iron.

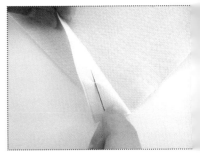

2 From the wrong side of the fold, make a small stitch, catching just a few threads of the fabric.

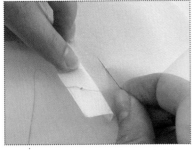

3 Then pick up just a single thread of the main fabric.

4 Reinsert your needle in the hem almost opposite to the stitch in step 2, approximately 5mm (¼in) further along.

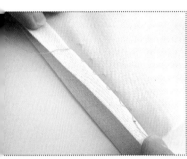

5 Repeat steps 3 and 4 along the whole hem, making your stitches as even as possible. The end result looks like a series of small triangles.

6 Pull gently on the thread every few stitches, so the two edges come together as the stitch is pulled tight.

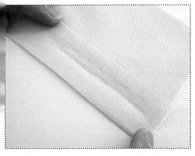

7 The stitches on the wrong side should be tiny...

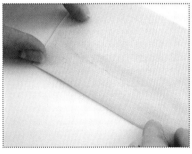

8 ...and the stitches on the right side almost invisible.

Catch stitch

What is it for?

Sometimes known as herringbone stitch, this stitch can be used
to hold a hem in place.

1 Bring your needle from the inside of the
hem to the outside.

2 Then reinsert in the main fabric just
above the edge of the hem. Bring out your
needle 5mm (¼in) behind the entry point.

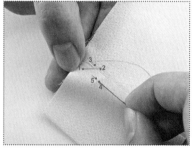

3 Pull gently and insert the needle back
into the hem, from front to back.

4 Reinsert it in the fabric and continue
again from step 2.

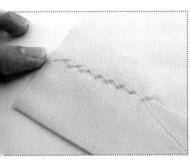

5 These crossed stitches form a catch stitch.

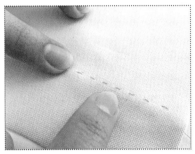

6 You should end up with straight, even stitching on the right side of the fabric.

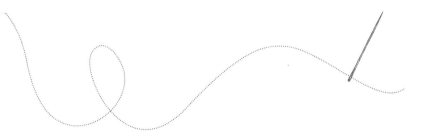

Seams

Basic seam

In dressmaking, this seam is often sewn with a 1 to 1.5cm (½ to ⅝in) seam allowance.

1 Take two pieces of fabric and place them right sides together, matching the raw edges of the fabric along the section to be sewn. Pin.

2 Stitch 1–1.5cm (½–⅝in) from the edge, depending on the pattern's stated stitch allowance. Use the lines engraved on the needle plate to guide you (first line next to the presser foot, marked 10, meaning 10mm).

3 Press the seam open.

4 You have completed your seam.

Flat-felled seam

This seam requires a 1.5cm (⅝in) seam allowance.

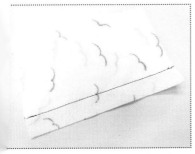

1 Take two pieces of fabric and place them right sides together. Pin, then stitch 1.5cm (⅝in) from the edge.

2 Press the seam allowances to one side. Trim one seam allowance to half the width.

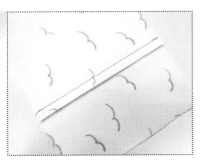

3 Fold the untrimmed seam allowance over and around the trimmed seam allowance, enclosing it inside. Top-stitch 5mm (¼in) away from the folded edge, through all layers of fabric.

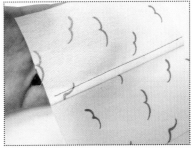

4 The result is a row of stitches parallel to the seamline on the right side of the fabric and a neat, strong finish on the wrong side.

Stitching a corner

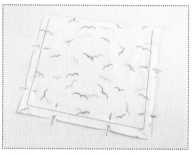

1 Prepare your fabric by drawing on your stitch margins to assist you as you sew.

2 Sew the seam as normal, up to the corners.

3 1cm (⅜in) before you reach the corner, stop sewing and lift up the presser foot. Make sure your needle is still in the fabric.

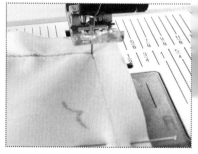

4 Raise the presser foot and pivot your fabric by 90 degrees.

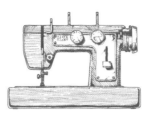

5 Lower the presser foot and continue stitching your next edge.

6 To ensure a nice finish, clip the corners at a 45-degree angle, making sure you don't cut through the stitching.

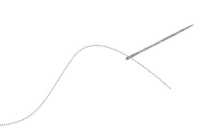

7 Turn your work the right way out and push out the corners carefully, using a capped pen if necessary.

French seam

Ideal for very lightweight or sheer fabrics. This seam requires a 1 to 1.5cm (½ to ⅝in) seam allowance.

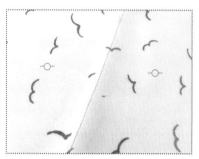

1 Take two pieces of fabric and place them wrong sides together. Pin and sew together 3mm (⅛in) from the edge (if the seam allowances are 1cm (⅜in)) or 5mm (¼in) from the edge (if the seam allowances are 1.5cm (⅝in)). Draw the stitch line on to the fabric, if it will help.

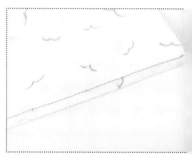

2 Press your seam allowances flat and to one side, fold the fabric right sides together, then pin. This time sew 5mm (¼in) from the edge (if the seam allowances are 1cm (⅜in)) or 1cm (⅜in) from the edge (if the seam allowances are 1.5cm (⅝in)).

3 Press. You now have a basic seam on the right side.

4 On the wrong side, the edge of the fabric is enclosed within the seam, giving an attractive finish.

Top-stitching

1 After you have sewn your fabric together and ironed it, you can sew to one side of the seam or a long it, both to embellish it and to help the seam lie flat.

2 Edge-stitching and 'stitching in the ditch' are two types of top-stitching. Edge-stitching is visible (at the collar, cuffs, button placket, waistband, and so on) and tends to be 3mm–1cm (⅛–⅜in) away from the seam.

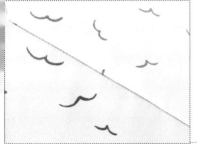

3 If you 'stitch in the ditch' (i.e. over the original seam), your stitches cannot be seen. It is more generally used for sewing a belt together, for example.

Hems

Hem

A hem is a folded edge at the bottom of a garment to make it neat and encase the raw edges. The seam allowance is often 3cm (1¼in) but it can be larger or smaller depending on the garment's finish.

Having prepared your hem by pressing an initial 1cm (⅜in) fold, then a 2cm (¾in) fold, pin to secure.

2 Position your fabric wrong side up. Stitch along the inner edge of the hem with the necessary seam allowance (see Tip, below, or refer to your pattern). The wrong side is now top-stitched...

3 ...and there is a hemline parallel to the edge of the fabric on the right side.

Tip

As a general rule, a finished hem is 3cm (1¼in) wide, so you can sew 2.5 or 2cm (1 or ¾in) from the edge (if the raw edge of the fabric is just overcast on the wrong side). If you want to make a hem with two folds, your finished hem will be 2cm (¾in) wide so you should sew 1.5cm (⅝in) from the edge.

Blind hem

A blind hem is a method of finishing a garment with no visible hem. It can be done on the machine using the blind hem stitch setting, but also by hand.

1 Prepare your hem by pressing with an iron and turning the edge of the fabric to the wrong side by your desired width.

2 Pinch your main fabric against the hem to create a fold.

3 Pin this fold into position, ensuring your fabric is lying flat on the work surface.

4 Fit your blind hem foot to your machine and set your machine to do blind hem stitch. Use the guide on the foot to position your fabric correctly.

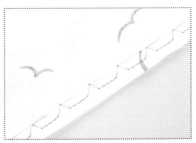

5 Your needle will create a straight line of stitches then triangles at regular intervals along the fold. Where the point of the triangle is formed, the tip of your needle should catch just a few threads of the edge of the fold.

6 When you have finished, you will have formed a zigzag pattern. This pattern will only be visible inside your hem.

7 After you have repositioned your hem correctly you will have zigzags on the wrong side of the garment...

8 ...and invisible stitching on the right side (you might just be able to see some tiny stitches on the fabric).

Rolled hem

A rolled hem is mostly used for finishing the edge of very lightweight fabrics (silks or cotton voile). They can also be stitched by hand, as is the case with the square silk scarves from a particular luxury brand.

1 Prepare the start of the hem by making an initial 5mm (¼in) fold in the fabric.

2 Make a second 5mm (¼in) fold.

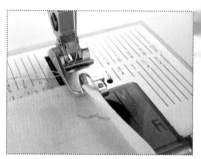

3 Install your rolled hem foot. Use the guide on the foot to insert your fabric correctly, wrong side facing down.

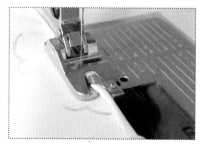

4 As you sew, the foot will ensure the hem forms all by itself.

5 You end up with a very neat, narrow hem.

Bias binding

Classic bias binding

Bias binding is used for finishing an edge but also to provide items with a neater, more secure finish. It is particularly used for finishing necklines or armholes as it allows curves to hold their shape far better than a classic hem.

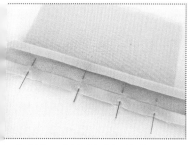

1 Unfold one fold of the bias binding. Pin the edge of the unfolded bias binding along the edge of the fabric, right sides together.

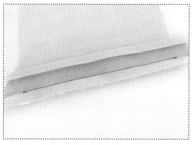

2 Sew along the fold mark of the bias.

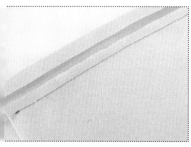

3 Press the seam allowance to the top with an iron.

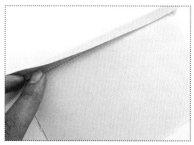

4 Fold the bias to the wrong side of the fabric to conceal the initial seam.

Classic bias binding

(continued from page 105)

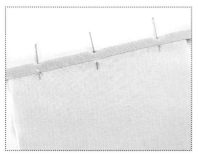

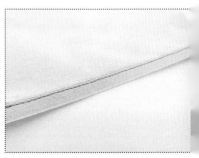

5 Pin into place, then top-stitch along the edge of the bias binding from the right side of the fabric.

6 Your bias binding is in place!

7 The top-stitching runs along the seam between the bias binding and the fabric on both sides.

Invisible bias binding

Invisible binding is ideal for the lightweight fabrics of, particularly women's, clothing precisely because it cannot be seen.

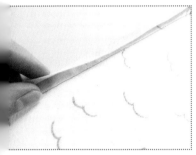

1 Follow steps 1–5 for classic bias binding (see pages 105–106), but don't top-stitch down the second side of the bias binding.

2 Turn the bias binding a second time towards the wrong side of the fabric so that it is no longer visible from the right side.

3 Pin, then top-stitch along the existing row of stitches, having drawn a line to help you stitch through the bias binding on the wrong side.

4 Your bias binding is in place! There is a single line of top-stitching on the right side, and the bias binding is only visible on the wrong side of the fabric.

Piping

Piping is a band of fabric encasing a cord that may come in various diameters. Piping is sewn between two pieces of fabric to provide a decorative finish on soft furnishings (cushion/pillow covers, for example) or to give a fancy finish to a piece of clothing.

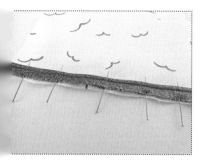

1 Pin the piping and one of your pieces of fabric right sides together, ensuring that the raw edge of the piping is aligned with the fabric edge. Make sure that the edge of the piping containing the cord is not the one that is aligned with the edge of the fabric. If necessary, tack (baste) so you do not have to take out pins as you sew, which can distort your stitching.

2 Use the zip (zipper) foot to help you sew the piping in place, as its shape allows you to stitch right up against the cord of the piping. Don't hesitate to adjust your needle position if you need to.

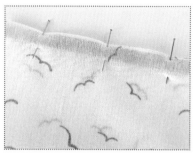

3 Lay your second piece of fabric over the first, aligning the edges and right sides together. The piping is now now sandwiched between the two pieces of fabric.

4 Sew the fabrics together along your initial row of stitches, again using the zip (zipper) foot.

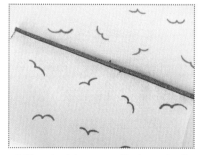

5 Turn the right way out. You have a lovely piped edge!

Ease

Distributing bulk using gathers

When you pin the top of a sleeve to the armhole of the body of the garment, you will find them to be different circumferences. There are various techniques to 'ease' this bulk, and one of the simplest is to use gathers.

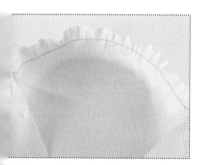

1 Sew a gathering stitch (see page 120) around the edge of the piece to be inserted into the garment.

2 Pull gently on the thread; this will gather the fabric, and pull in the excess material.

3 You can use your finger or thumbnail to even out the gathers and shape the piece (here, a sleeve). Be careful that you do not create folds.

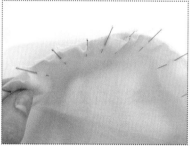

4 Pin the piece to the garment (here, the sleeve to the armhole), using the marker notches for alignment. Pin and sew the seam together.

Distributing bulk without using gathers

The second technique for distributing the excess fabric uses pins. A game of patience

1 Without sewing a row of stitches to create gathers, your first step is to match the top of your sleeve to the armhole using the marker notches.

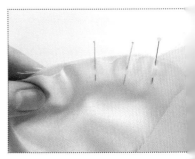

2 The bottom of the sleeve can be pinned immediately as the excess fabric should be distributed across the top of the sleeve to enable freedom of movement in the shoulder

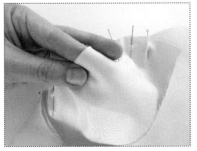

3 Then pin your fabric between the notches marking the back and top of the sleeve, ensuring that you distribute the surplus material evenly in a series of little 'waves'.

Two techniques:
1. The fabric stretches a little when it is cut in a curve; use the fingers of one hand to gently stretch the material on the armhole, while using your thumbs to push on the fabric on the sleeve side.
2. Alternatively, use your finger to create a 'roll' in the fabric on top, distributing the fabric waves. When you let go, there will be small waves between your pins, but when you sew you can pull them flat by gently stretching your fabric.

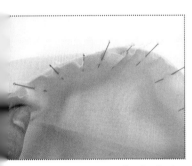

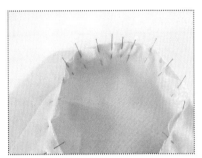

4 Repeat the same process for distributing the surplus fabric between the notch at the top of the sleeve and the front.

5 Pin and tack (baste) if necessary, then sew together on the machine.

Pleats and darts

Flat pleat

A flat pleat is easy to make and will enable you to create a series of folds or add volume to skirts, dresses and blouses.

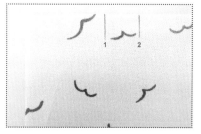

1 Pleats are marked on a pattern by notches with an arrow showing the direction of the pleat. Transfer the notches to the fabric and ensure that you have the arrow pointing in the same direction.

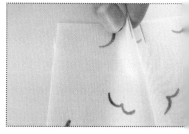

2 Keeping the fabric face up, pinch your fabric at the first notch (the one that will be folded to the second).

3 Keeping hold of the fabric, take it to the second notch. Flatten and pin. You can form several in a row for a full pleated effect.

4 Sew a seam 5mm (¼in) from the edge of the top of the fabric to hold the pleat(s) in place.

Box pleat

A box pleat is formed from two flat pleats facing each other.

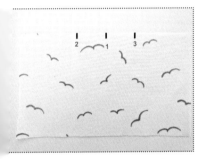

1 This time, on the pattern you will have three notches to help you create a box pleat. Transfer the notches to the fabric.

2 Keeping the fabric face up, pinch your fabric at notch no. 2 and bring it to notch no. 1. Flatten the fabric then pin to hold this first fold in place.

3 Now pinch the fabric at notch no. 3 and bring it to notch no. 1. Flatten the fabric then pin to hold this second fold in place.

4 You now have a box pleat as you might find on a skirt. Sew a seam 5mm (¼in) from the edge of the top of the fabric to hold your box pleat in place.

Inverted pleat

An inverted pleat is simply two flat pleats facing in opposite directions. You generally find them on the back of shirts and blouses.

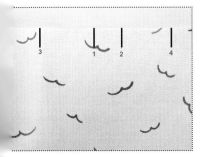

1 This time, on the pattern you will have four notches to help you create an inverted pleat. Transfer the notches to the fabric.

2 Keeping the fabric face up, pinch your fabric at notch no. 1 and bring it to notch no. 3.

3 Flatten the fabric then pin to hold this first fold in place.

4 Now pinch the fabric at notch no. 2 and bring it to notch no. 4. Flatten the fabric then pin to hold this second fold in place.

5 You now have an inverted pleat as you might find on the back of men's shirts. Sew a seam 0.5cm (¼in) from the edge of the top of the fabric to hold your inverted pleat in place.

Darts

A dart is used to take in a section of fabric in a garment to follow the contours of the body. It is particularly used for women's clothing at the bust or hips, but also to shape waists with contour darts.

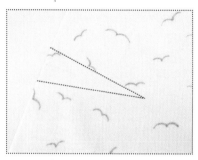

1 A standard dart is the type you will find most often in dressmaking patterns. Using carbon paper and the tracing wheel, transfer the dart marked on the pattern to the wrong side of your fabric.

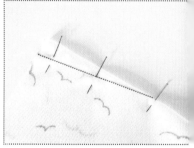

2 Fold your fabric right sides together, aligning both sides of your dart. Pin your fabric up to the point of the dart, ensuring that the markings are properly aligned.

3 Sew from the edge of the fabric to the point of your dart.

4 Press the dart flat on both sides.

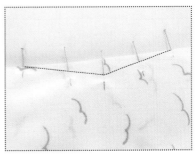

5 A similar technique is used for a contour dart, which is positioned right in the middle of a piece of fabric (usually at the waist of a garment).

6 Fold your fabric right sides together, aligning the ends of your dart, then sew.

7 Press with an iron on both sides.

Gathers

Gathers are a very simple dressmaking technique that can be used to create a particular look on a garment, form smocking or draw up excess fabric.

1 To make gathers, you first need to sew a straight line 1cm (⅜in) from the edge of your fabric. Use long stitches (stitch length 4) with no backstitching at the beginning or end. Depending on your garment, you may need to sew a second line, 1cm (⅜in) below the first. Use the same straight stitch and stitch length as before.

2 Take hold of the threads at the one end of your rows of stitching, your fabric right side up. Then pull gently to create gathers. Distribute them as you wish.

Buttonholes

**To make a buttonhole, check whether your machine
has an automatic buttonhole function.
Automatic buttonholes are represented by a single
rectangle on the stitch selector, whereas manual
buttonholes are represented by three rectangles.**

Regardless of what machine you have, always test your buttonhole on
a scrap of your chosen fabric, to make sure you're happy with placement
and sizing.

✳ ✳ ✳ *Warning!* ✳ ✳ ✳
*On electronic machines: you simply
need to select the buttonhole stitch
and have the foot attachment for
automatic buttonholing.*

*On mechanical machines: you need
to check whether it has automatic
buttonholing depending on whether you
have the right foot. You also need to think
about turning the stitch length selector to
the buttonhole symbol and selecting 6 for
the stitch width.*

Manual buttonholing

Mark the buttonhole opening on your fabric. It is represented by a straight line equal to the diameter of your button + 3 to 5mm (⅛ to ¼in).

• Fit your buttonhole foot on your sewing machine.
• Check the stitch selector to see in which order the machine will run so you can position the opening of the presser foot correctly.

To simplify, check the direction of the buttonhole diagrams on your sewing machine. Example:

1. fabric feeds away from you (left-hand edge)
2. end of rectangle farthest away from you
3. fabric feeds towards you (right-hand edge)
4. end of the rectangle closest to you, end point.

The order is not the same on all machines, so make sure to check your user manual.

• Then start from position no. 1, stopping when you reach the end of your line. Use the hand wheel to lift the needle manually.
• Turn the stitch selector to position 2. Go backwards and forwards a few times, then lift the needle manually using the wheel.
• Turn the stitch selector to 3 to sew the other edge of the buttonhole, then lift the needle manually using the wheel.
• Finally, reposition the stitch selector to 4 (the same as for position 2) and sew to complete the outside of the buttonhole by going backwards and forwards a few times.

Automatic buttonholing

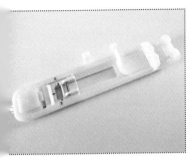

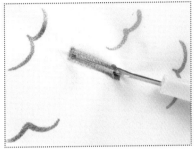

No need to draw on the buttonhole;
simply pop your button into the recess
in the buttonhole foot.
Drop the handle to the side of the
needle threader. Then push it backwards
as shown above.
Turn the stitch selector to buttonhole
stitch, then press the pedal.
It will make the buttonhole all by itself!

For both methods, you will need to
snip the finished buttonhole open
using a seam ripper (as above) or some
embroidery scissors.

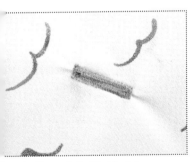

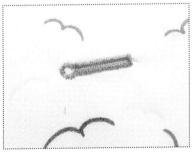

Standard buttonhole, ideal for light- to
medium-weight fabrics.

Keyhole buttonhole, ideal for heavy-weight,
non-stretch fabrics.

Zips (zippers)

Open-ended zip (zipper)

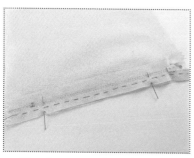

1 Align the closed zip (zipper) right sides together with the edge of the fabric. Pin into place, then tack (baste) in placex.

2 It is easiest if you begin your seam at the end of the zip (zipper) opposite the zip (zipper) pull. Identify the side on which you need to position the needle in relation to the presser foot: to the left or to the right. Then insert the special zip (zipper) foot accordingly.

3 The zip (zipper) foot runs alongside the teeth of the zip (zipper). Sew along the length, stopping when you reach the pull. Keep the needle inserted through the fabric so you can lift the presser foot.

Slide the zip (zipper) pull backwards to move it out of the way.

5 Before you carry on sewing, don't forget to lower the presser foot again.

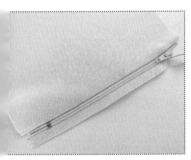

Fold back the zip (zipper) and press. You have attached the first side of the zip (zipper).

7 Align the other side of the zip (zipper) with the raw edge of a second piece of fabric, right sides together.

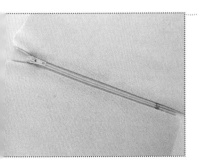

8 Follow the same steps as you did for the first side. Turn the right way out and press. You can also top-stitch along either side of the zip (zipper) if you wish.

Lapped zip (zipper)

This method allows you to conceal the teeth of the zip (zipper) without the need for an invisible zip (zipper).

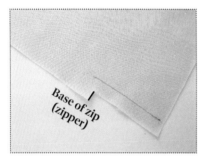

Base of zip (zipper)

1 Mark out where your zip (zipper) will sit on your fabric. If your zip will be shorter than the seam it's being stitched int mark the base of the zip. A lapped zip has a wider-than-usual seam allowance, which corresponds with the width of the zip. With a 2cm (¾in) seam allowance, sew your two pieces of fabric right sides together with a regular stitch length, until you reach the bas of the zip; then continue to sew 1.5cm (⅝in) beyond this point. Below the base of the zip trim away 5mm (¼in) of the seam allowance

2 Then sew the rest of this opening together using long stitches (so you can unpick them easily later).

3 Press the seams open along the full length of the seam. Position the right side of the zip (zipper) against the seam of the opening, the teeth of the zip (zipper) in the centre, aligned with the seam. Pin, then tack (baste) the zip (zipper) in place.

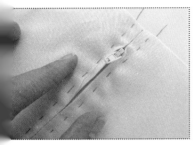

4 Unpick some of the long stitches of the seam so you can open the zip (zipper) and move the zip (zipper) pull out of the way before the next stage.

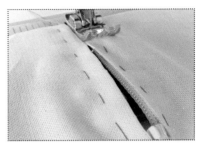

5 Start sewing one side of the zip (zipper), 1cm (⅜in) from the centre seam, as far as the base of the zip (zipper).

6 Move the zip (zipper) pull as you are sewing, keeping the needle through the fabric as you lift the presser foot.

7 At the base of the zip (zipper), pivot 90 degrees and sew a perpendicular seam for 1.5cm (⅝in).

8 Pivot another 90 degrees and sew back up the other side of the zip (zipper), still 1cm (⅜in) from the centre seam.

9 Completely unpick the temporary seam made in step 2, so you can open and close the zip (zipper).

Invisible zip (zipper)

For this type of zip (zipper) you will need an 'invisible zip tape', which is different fro_
standard zips: the zip (zipper) teeth are on the wrong side, and the zip (zipper) pull
is shaped like a drop of water. This type of zip (zipper) is used on dresses, skirts and
trousers with side openings.

1 Align one edge of the zip (zipper) with the edge of the fabric, right sides together. Pin up to the marker notch and tac_ (baste) into place to make machine-stitchin_ the seam simpler. Attach the invisible zip (zipper) foot to the sewing machine. Positio_ the fabric under the foot, and use your finge_ to ease the zip (zipper) teeth away from the tape so you can position them in the correct tunnel of the foot.

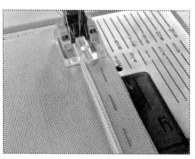

2 Stitch along the full length.

3 Come to a halt when you reach the zip (zipper) pull; it is not like an open-ended zip (zipper) in that you cannot pull it past the presser foot. Consequently, you have to stop here.

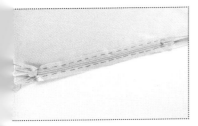

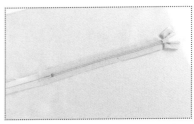

4 Repeat on the other side of the zip (zipper), ensuring that it does not roll itself up. The simplest method is to pin it into place while keeping the zip closed.

5 Once the other side of the zip (zipper) is sewn in, close it again and press the seam open to prepare for sewing the base of the zip.

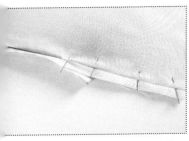

6 Pin the fabric right sides together as far as the zip (zipper) seam.

7 Sew along the pinned edge from step 6 with a universal zip (zipper) foot, up to the zip (zipper) seam, trying to get as close as possible to the seam.

8 Hand sew the end of the zip (zipper) tape into place to prevent the pull from coming off. Turn the right way out and press with an iron.

9 When finished, you will not be able see the zip (zipper) teeth anymore!

Necklines and openings

Facing (rounded and V-shaped)

Rounded neckline

The secret of an attractive rounded neckline and well-positioned facing? Clip the fabric at regular intervals!

1 Pin your facing piece to the neckline of your garment right sides together. Stitch 1cm (⅜in) from the edge then clip into the seam allowance to add ease.

2 Fold the facing to the wrong side of the garment, then press.

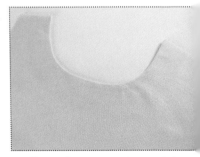

3 You now have an attractive rounded neckline!

V-shaped facing

This is not too complicated. Draw the angle at the bottom of the
'V' perfectly accurately to help you sew a perfect seam. Once again,
the secret is to clip the edges up to the point where the seams meet.

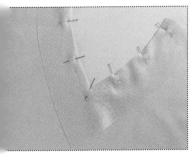

1 Pin your facing to the neckline of your garment right sides together. Draw on the angle formed at the bottom of the 'V' of your neckline, as deep as your seam allowance.

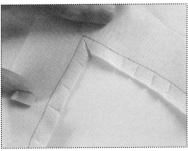

2 Sew 1cm (⅜in) from the edge, pivoting at the angle (see page 96). Clip your seam allowances up to the point of the 'V'.

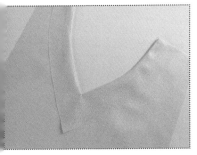

3 Fold the facing to the wrong side of the garment, then press.

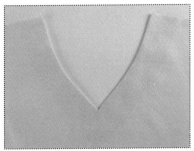

4 You now have an attractive V-shaped neckline!

Reinforced vent

This is often used at the back of the neckline on children's clothes to make the garment easier to take off, and prevent it from tearing. You will also find similar slits on the cuffs of blouses where the bottom of the sleeve is tight.

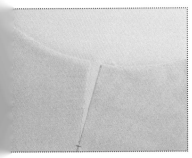

Mark the length of the slit-opening on the garment. Cut along your line.

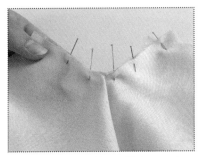

2 Pin your piece of facing fabric around the full length of this opening, right sides together.

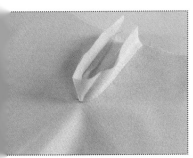

3 Sew the facing to the fabric with a 1cm (⅜in) seam, trying not to create a fold at the angle formed by the cut in the fabric.

4 Fold the facing to the wrong side of the main fabric. Turn under the unstitched edge by 5mm (¼in).

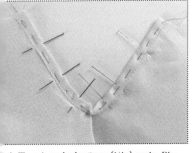

5 Turn it under by 5mm (¼in) again. Pin and tack (baste) in place.

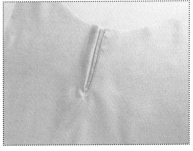

6 Top-stitch, then press with an iron to give your faced slit its final shape.

Tunisian neckline

Essential for a garment with no other opening so it is easy to slip on over your head. It can stay open or have buttons. When it has buttons, it is known as a polo placket it is shorter and ends in a point.

1 Mark the length of the opening on the garment. Draw an outline around this opening, at a distance of 1cm (⅜in). From the base of the opening, draw diagonal lines that reach the bottom-left and -right corners, creating a triangle.

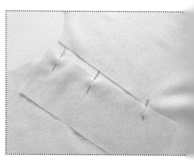

2 Position the plackets either side of the opening, right sides together.

3 Stitch 1cm (⅜in) from the edge, stopping when you reach the end of the opening.

4 Cut into the little diagonal lines you drew earlier, creating a triangular notch in the seam allowance (known as a swallow tail).

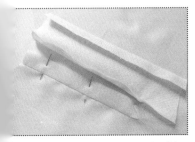

Fold one placket to the wrong side of the fabric, leaving a 1cm (⅜in) fold visible the right side of the fabric. This is the ck placket.

6 The back placket will slip perfectly under the little triangle.

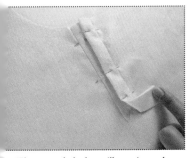

7 The second placket will remain on the right side of the fabric and will conceal the triangle. Turn under the raw edge by 1cm ⅜in), then fold the whole placket in half, ncasing the stitched raw edge.

8 Top-stitch along the folds of both plackets.

9 Turn under the short bottom ends of both plackets by 1cm (⅜in) on both right side and wrong side and sew down, forming a rectangle with a cross in the centre.

Collars

Stand-up collar

A stand-up collar is the easiest to sew. You simply need to cut two collar pieces first

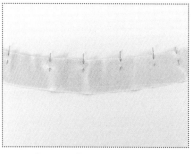

1 Pin the two collar pieces right sides together.

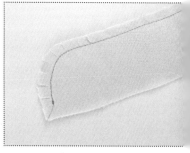

2 Sew 1cm (⅜in) from the edge around th top, then clip the curves.

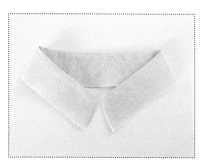

3 Turn the right way out and press with an iron.

Flat collar

A flat collar is likewise fairly simple to sew, you simply need to make sure you are forming the curves neatly.

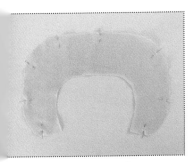

Pin the two collar pieces right sides together.

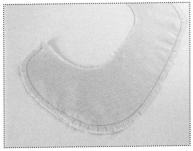

2 Stitch 1cm (⅜in) along the lower edge, carefully following the curves of the collar. Then clip all round your seam.

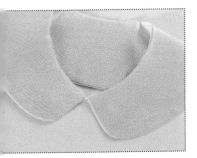

3 Turn the right way out and press with an iron.

Shirt collar

A shirt collar is a little more technical. It comprises two collar stand pieces and two lapel pieces.

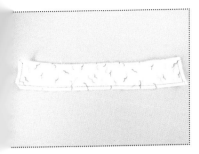

1 Pin the two lapel pieces right sides together. Stitch 1cm (⅜in) along the bottom edge, forming neat points at the angle of the lapels.

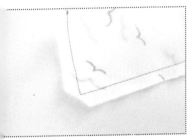

2 Clip the corners.

3 Turn the right way out and press the lapels. Crease or mark the centres of the lapels and stand pieces to help you to pin them together correctly. The lapels should be 'sandwiched' between the two stand pieces which should be right sides together.

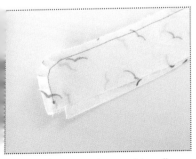

4 Sew along top and curve of the collar stands, 1cm (⅜in) from the edge. Clip the curves.

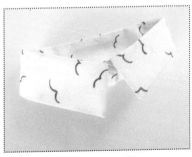

5 Turn the right way out and press.

Pockets

Patch pocket with a flap

Patch pockets, with or without a flap, will give a more casual or sporty look to your garments.

To help you fold your seam allowances you can make a template (such as a thick piece of card) that is the final size of the pocket.

1 Pin your pocket flaps right sides together. Stitch 1cm (⅜in) from the edge then clip the corners. Turn the right way out.

2 Turn under a 1cm (⅜in) hem along the top of the pocket. Sew in place along the bottom of the fold.

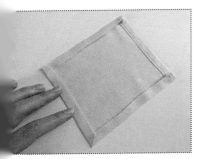

3 Turn under 1cm (⅜in) seam allowances on the remaining three sides of the pocket.

4 Position your pocket on your garment. Pin.

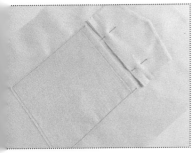

5 Top-stitch round the three sides of your pocket. Then position your flap 1cm (⅜in) above it.

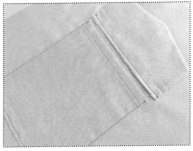

6 Stitch the bottom edge of the flap in place with a 5mm (¼in) seam allowance

7 Press the flap towards and over the pocket, then stitch along the top edge of the flap with a 1cm (⅜in) seam allowance. This last seam 'traps' the seam allowance in step 6; if you can still see a few threads poking through the hem, snip them off with embroidery scissors.

In-seam pocket

These pockets are 'invisible' and concealed in the garment's side seams.

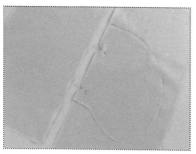

1 Position your two main pieces of fabric right side up. Match one pocket from a pair with the notches on its corresponding main fabric piece, its right side facing up. Repeat with the other pocket and fabric piece; you should have mirrored pockets and main fabric pieces.

2 Stitch 1cm (⅜in) from the edge of both pockets, stopping before the start and end of the markers.

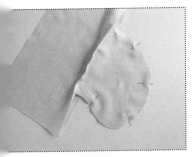

3 Fold the pockets away from the main fabric. Pin the main fabric to main fabric and pocket to pocket, right sides together.

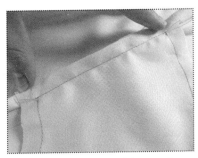

4 Sew the pockets around the curved edges only, together with a 1cm (⅜in) seam allowance, starting and finishing at the original seam.

5 Sew up the seam of the main fabric pieces, right sides together, above and below the pocket, 1cm (⅜in) from the edge.

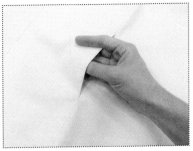

6 Turn the right way out and press with an iron. You have now completed the in-seam pockets.

Hip pocket

These pockets are mostly associated with trousers.
They are called rounded pockets when they run in a curve and diagonal pockets when
the top seam is straight.

1 Align pocket lining no. 1 right sides together with the main fabric piece that has the pocket cut out. Pin, right sides together, then stitch 1cm (⅜in) from the edge. Clip in to the seam allowance.

2 Fold the two pieces, wrong sides together, and press with an iron.

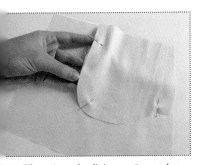

3 Then pin pocket lining no. 2 to pocket lining no. 1, right sides together. Sew the two pocket pieces together around the curved edge only.

4 Turn the pocket pieces right sides out. You have your pocket!

Piped pocket

These are the most complicated pockets to do – you need to be very accurate as every millimetre counts.

These pockets are often found on the back of tailored trousers, or on jackets and coats.

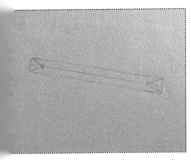

Mark the pocket opening (centre lines). Mark a 1cm (⅜in) outline all around the ⸱cket opening line, then draw a 'V' at each ⸱d of the pocket-opening line that extends ⸱o the corners of the outline.

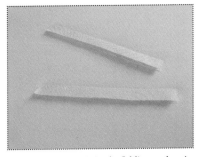

2 Prepare your piping by folding each strip in half lengthways, wrong sides together.

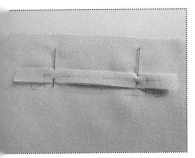

3 Pin each folded piping strip either side of the pocket-opening line, with the raw ⸱dges matching the drawn line. The piping ⸱nds extend beyond each side of the drawn ⸱ox; this is quite correct! In our example, the ⸱pening is 10cm (4in) long while the piping ⸱ieces measure 12cm (4¾in).

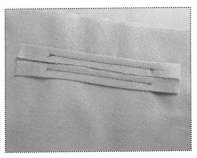

4 Stitch halfway down the piping pieces, stopping when you reach the points of your 'V's.

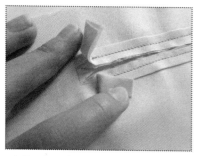

5 Cut along the pocket-opening lines and the diagonal lines of each 'V'.

6 Turn your piping pieces to the wrong side (inside) of the garment, forming a beautiful, piped opening.

7 On the wrong side, pin your first pocket lining piece to the top piping piece, raw edges together and the wrong side of the pocket lining facing up. Sew in place.

8 Do the same with the second pocket lining piece on the bottom piping piece You are still working on the wrong side (inside) of the garment.

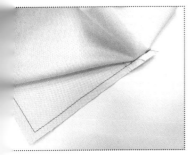

Then pin the two pocket lining pieces
right sides together along the side seams
bottom seam, trapping the triangles on
her side of the opening.

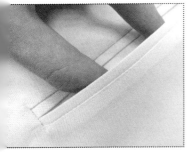

0 Sew together, then press the pocket
from the right side.

INDEX

Backstitch, backstitching 8, 23, 86–87, 120

Bias binding 88, 105–107

Bobbin 8, 12–13, 16–21, 29, 30, 33

Buttonhole(s) 25, 26, 27, 36, 38, 41, 79, 121–123

Collar(s) 71, 72, 99, 136–139

Corner(s) 78, 96–97, 134, 139, 140, 147

Cutting 38–39, 73, 78, 79, 80–81

Darts 40, 79, 114, 118–119

Embroidery 39, 55, 123, 141

Facing(s) 78, 130–133

Fusible binding, see also: interfacing 70–72

Gathers 110–112, 120

Hem 24, 25, 26, 37, 41, 71, 78, 88, 90–92, 100–105, 140, 141

Interfacing, see also: fusible binding 64, 70–73

Knit(s), knitted 24, 32, 33, 46, 47, 50, 57, 67, 72

Lining 67, 70–71, 73, 145, 148

Needle(s) 8, 10, 11, 15, 16, 21, 22, 26, 28, 29, 32–33, 35, 85, 86, 88, 90, 92, 94, 96, 103, 109, 122–123, 124, 127

Pleats 114–117

Pockets 140–148

Presser foot 10, 15, 21, 31, 36–37, 94, 96, 97, 122, 124, 125, 127, 128, 137

Skirt(s) 53, 57, 60, 69, 73, 78, 114, 115, 128

Spool 8, 13, 14, 33

Stretch 24, 25, 32, 47, 50, 51, 57, 69, 7: 78, 112

Tension 8, 15, 17, 19, 27, 29, 78

Threading 12–22, 24, 29, 30

Trousers 43, 53–55, 59, 65, 69, 73, 76, 128, 144, 146

Warp and weft 47, 48, 50, 54, 56, 60

Washing 53–57, 59–61, 63–65, 67–69, 78

Zigzag 24, 25, 26, 33, 78, 103

Zip (zipper) 36, 109, 124–129

Acknowledgements

Particular thanks go to Mélanie Jean and the whole team at Mango Editions who support me in the writing world.

A massive thank you to Fabrice, Sonia and Pretty Mercerie.

A wink to my students for their encouragement and some wonderful sewing sessions at my various different workshops.

And above all, an enormous thanks to my family and the people who support me in my passion, behind the scenes.

First published in the UK in 2025 by
Search Press Limited
Wellwood, North Farm Road,
Tunbridge Wells, Kent TN2 3DR

© First published in French by Mango,
Paris, France – 2019, as *Petit précis de couture*.

English translation by Burravoe Translation Services

Direction: Guillaume Pô
Editor: Tatiana Delesalle
Publisher: Mélanie Jean
Art direction: Chloé Eve
Page-setting: Johanna Fritz
Illustrations: Laure Guyet
Photographs and styling on pages 4, 6–7, 44–45, 82–83:
Fabrice Besse and Sonia Roy

ISBN: 978-1-80092-257-0
ebook ISBN: 978-1-80093-256-2

Suppliers
If you have difficulty in obtaining any of the materials and equipment mentioned in this book, then please visit the Search Press website for details of suppliers:
www.searchpress.com

Bookmarked Hub
For further ideas and inspiration, and to join our free online community, visit www.bookmarkedhub.com

MIX
Paper | Supporting responsible forestry
FSC
www.fsc.org
FSC® C136333